FIRST AMERICANS
The Choctaw

SARAH De CAPUA

Marshall Cavendish
Benchmark
New York

ACKNOWLEDGMENTS

Series consultant: Raymond Bial

Marshall Cavendish
99 White Plains Road
Tarrytown, New York 10591-5502
www.marshallcavendish.us

Library of Congress Cataloging-in-Publication Data
De Capua, Sarah.
The Choctaw / by Sarah De Capua.
p. cm.
Summary: "Provides comprehensive information on the background,
lifestyle, beliefs, and present-day lives of the Choctaw people"
—Provided by publisher.
Includes bibliographical references and index.
ISBN 978-0-7614-3018-6
1. Choctaw Indians—History—Juvenile literature.   2. Choctaw
Indians—Social life and customs—Juvenile literature.   I. Title.
E99.C8D44 2009
973.04'97—dc22
2007033727

Front cover: A part-Choctaw girl and her Navaho friend wearing their regalia at the Red Earth Festival, Oklahoma City
Title page: Baskets made by members of the Mississippi Band of Choctaw Indians
Photo research by: Connie Gardner
Cover photo by Peter Turnley/CORBIS
The photographs in this book are used by permission and through the courtesy of: *Raymond Bial:* 1; *Nativestock.com:* Marilyn "Angel" Wynn, 4, 14, 16, 18, 19, 24, 25, 34; *North Wind:* 7, 8, 33; *The Granger Collection:* 12; *Corbis:* Malcolm Hanes, 26; Bettmann, 29; *Getty Images:* Shelly Katz, 36; Alex Wong, 40; *Associated Press:* 38; Rogelio Sohs, 39; *The Philbrook Museum of Art, Inc.:* Chief Terry Saul, Choctaw Bone Picker Ceremony, 1951, Museum Purchase, 1951.12, c 2007 The Philbrook Museum of Art, Inc. Tulsa, Oklahoma.

Editor: Deborah Grahame
Publisher: Michelle Bisson
Art Director: Anahid Hamparian
Series Designer: Symon Chow

Printed in Malaysia
1 3 5 6 4 2

CONTENTS

1 · WHO ARE THE CHOCTAW PEOPLE?

Choctaw Indians live in communities in southeastern Oklahoma and Louisiana, and on reservations in Mississippi and Alabama. Choctaw people also live beside their non-Indian neighbors in cities and towns throughout the United States.

The Choctaw call themselves the *Chata* or *Okla Chahta*. *Okla* is the Choctaw word for "people," "tribe," or "nation." *Chata* was the name of one of the tribe's leaders. The name *Choctaw* comes from the Creek word *chate*, which means "red."

Before 1700 the Choctaw lived in the southern part of what later became the United States, in the area that is now southeast Louisiana, Mississippi, and western Alabama. To

A view of river cane on Choctaw land

the southwest lived the Natchez Indians, in present-day Louisiana. Northwest of the Choctaw were the Quapaw of modern Arkansas. The Chickasaw, who may have had the same **ancestors** as the Choctaw, lived to the North, in today's Mississippi and Alabama. The Choctaw were one of the tribes that came to be known as the Five Civilized Tribes. The Cherokee, Creek, Seminole, and Chickasaw were also members of this group.

Early Choctaw moved seasonally, traveling as they hunted and fished for food and gathered wild plants. Around 900 C.E. the Choctaw learned how to grow corn, which became their most important crop. The soil and climate were good for growing crops. So the Choctaw stopped living as nomads and built settled communities. They traded with other tribes in the Southeast. Trade goods included beaver and bear **pelts**, buffalo hides, bear oil, seashells, freshwater pearls, and copper. The Choctaw sometimes traded extra corn after the harvest.

European explorers first reached the present-day southeastern United States in 1539. The Spanish explorer Hernando de Soto led a group looking for gold and silver. Fighting broke out between de Soto's men and various groups of Native Americans.

De Soto's expedition meets Native Americans on the Mississippi River in 1542.

In the late 1600s the French claimed the vast lands along the Mississippi River, which they called Louisiana. To bring about good relations with the Choctaw, the French traded metal tools, wool blankets, and other goods for animal skins and furs. The French established the cities of New Orleans, Louisiana; Mobile, Alabama; and Biloxi, Mississippi. In 1729

An encampment of French fur traders

French traders offered the Choctaw 800 pounds (363 kilograms) of gifts that included clothing, blankets, wool, guns and gunpowder, and hatchets. That same year the Choctaw helped the French defeat a group of Natchez Indians who had been fighting the French for several months.

From the French, the Choctaw adopted certain tools and practices that changed the Choctaw way of life. They raised cattle, pigs, poultry, and horses. Eventually they developed a breed of horse that became known as the Choctaw pony. Some Choctaw became wealthy by running trading posts. Marriages took place between non-Indians and Choctaw, usually between Choctaw women and traders.

Conflicts broke out between French and English settlers. From 1754 to 1763 the two sides fought the French and Indian War. The Choctaw supported France, but did not fight against the English. After the English won the war, the Choctaw continued to live where they were already settled. A few Choctaw who were living outside of Louisiana moved their villages there to be near the French.

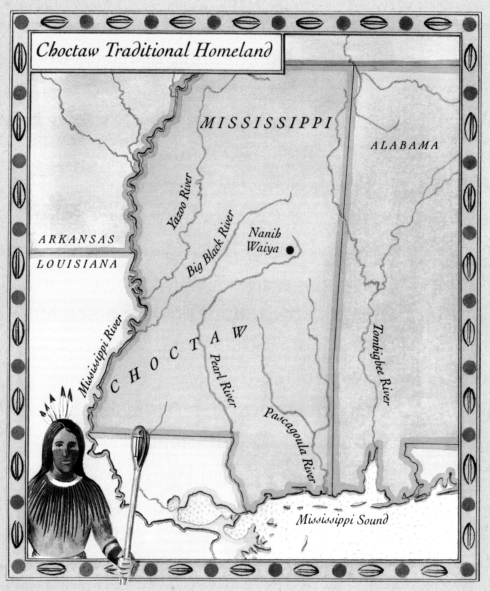

This map shows the traditional homeland of the Choctaw.

As more English settlers arrived, many Choctaw and other Native Americans caught deadly new diseases. Smallpox and measles killed many Choctaw, whose bodies lacked the natural ability to fight them off.

By the 1770s the American colonists began to fight for independence from Great Britain. The Choctaw lived outside of the thirteen colonies and did not fight for either side in the Revolutionary War (1775–1783). After the Americans won the war the Choctaw signed a treaty with the U.S. government. In the 1801 treaty the Choctaw gave more than 2.6 million acres (1.1 million hectares) of land to the United States.

The Choctaw signed another treaty in 1803, giving even more land to the United States. Also in 1803, President Thomas Jefferson bought land that had previously been controlled by France. It is known as the Louisiana Purchase. The purchase added 827,987 square miles (2,144,476 square kilometers) to the United States. The territory extended north to

Pushmataha

Remembered today as the greatest of all Choctaw chiefs, Pushmataha was born in 1764, near present-day Macon, Mississippi. Beginning at a young age he learned to fight against the Choctaw enemies, the Creek Indians. By the time he was an adult, Pushmataha was a respected warrior and chief. Pushmataha became a skilled public speaker and **diplomat** for the Choctaw. He took part in the Fort Confederation meeting held in 1802, which resulted in a treaty between the Choctaw and the United States.

Pushmataha (1764–1824)

Afterward Pushmataha played an important role in all meetings and treaties between the Choctaw and the U.S. government. When Creek Indians killed more than five hundred Americans at Fort Mims, in present-day Alabama, Pushmataha once again battled the Creek Indians when he organized a Choctaw military force to assist the U.S. Army in fighting them.

In 1824 Pushmataha and other chiefs went to Washington, D.C., to obtain payments from the U.S. government in exchange for land that the government wanted to give the Indians. During his trip to Washington, Pushmataha became ill and died. He was honored with a military funeral and is buried in the Congressional Cemetery in Washington, D.C. A tall marble monument marks his grave. His portrait hangs in the Hall of Fame of the state of Mississippi in Jackson, the state capital.

south from Canada to the Gulf of Mexico, and east to west from the Mississippi River to the Rocky Mountains. It would later be divided into all or parts of fifteen U.S. states. Thousands more settlers moved through or onto Choctaw lands.

Between 1803 and 1830 the Choctaw signed five more treaties with the U.S. government, giving up more of their land. When the U.S. Congress passed the Indian Removal Act in 1830, the eastern tribes were required to move to Indian Territory (now Oklahoma). That same year Choctaw leaders signed the Treaty of Dancing Rabbit Creek. The treaty required the Choctaw to turn over their remaining land to the U.S. government. In exchange, the Choctaw would move to Indian Territory.

The journey west, first of the Choctaw and then of the other members of the Five Civilized Tribes, became known as the Trail of Tears. Between 1831 and 1838 a total of about 50,000 people set out on horseback, in wagons, and on foot

This painting of Indians along the Trail of Tears was created by a Native American artist.

for Indian Territory. Many died of illness, cold, or hunger during the long journey.

About one thousand of the four thousand Choctaw in Mississippi would not leave their homeland. They lived in a sparsely populated area and hoped U.S. government officials would not find them and force them out. Meanwhile, over time, the Choctaw in Indian Territory set up their own tribal government and wrote a constitution that established laws for the tribe. But they suffered from poverty, a lack of jobs and education, and poor health care.

In the 1880s Indian Territory became the home of increasing numbers of settlers, called homesteaders. In 1907 Indian Territory became the state of Oklahoma. Around that time, oil was discovered there, which led to the arrival of more settlers. Even though the Choctaw were citizens of Oklahoma, they continued to face hardships. Their struggles were not eased after Congress granted U.S. citizenship to all Native Americans in 1924.

By the mid- to late-twentieth century, however, Congress had passed laws to improve the lives of Native Americans. In the 1980s and 1990s the Choctaw and other Native American tribes established several businesses and modern industries. These businesses and industries continue to be successful in the twenty-first century.

2 · LIFE IN THE SOUTHEAST

Choctaw villages were located near rivers or streams. Walls or **moats** surrounded the villages to protect the inhabitants from enemies. Each village was made up of two hundred to three hundred houses. Houses were made from wood, thatch, bark, or reeds. Each family usually had two homes: a summer home and a winter home.

Summer homes were made from loosely woven mats. The holes in the mats allowed fresh air to flow into the home. The home had separate areas for cooking and sleeping.

Winter homes were made by weaving saplings together and packing a mixture of grass and clay into the cracks to keep out the cold.

The roofs of both kinds of homes were made of thatch. A hole was cut in them to allow the smoke from cooking fires to

This is an example of a Choctaw winter home.

escape. Choctaw homes and the items inside—baskets, bowls, clothing, tools, and weapons—were considered to be the women's property.

Choctaw families were made up of a father, a mother, and their children. Every family member had a job. Men were farmers, warriors, fishermen, traders, **shamans**, and tribal leaders. They cleared fields and planted crops of corn, beans,

Corn, beans, and squash were among the most important crops to the Choctaw.

squash, potatoes, pumpkins, and melons. Men hunted deer, bears, rabbits, squirrels, and beavers for meat. They also hunted wild turkeys and other birds, and fished in nearby rivers and streams. Men made tools and weapons, built canoes, sewed moccasins, and crafted drums. They built their families' homes.

Choctaw women were responsible for household chores, caring for the children, tending the crops, and for storing and preparing food. They picked fruits and berries that grew in the forests. They prepared animal hides and made them into clothing and blankets. After the arrival of the Europeans, they wove fabric for use as clothing and blankets. The women

The Europeans introduced weaving looms like this one, which the Choctaw used to make cloth.

Sweet Corn Bread

Corn was the most important crop for the Choctaw. It was prepared in a variety of ways, including being roasted, boiled, or stewed with meats and vegetables. Choctaw women made corn flour by placing corn kernels in a wooden bowl, or in the "bowl" of a hollowed-out log, and using a large stone to grind the kernels into powder. The corn flour was then used to make breads and cakes.

This corn bread includes ingredients that were not available to the Choctaw, but the bread is similar to the kind they made. Ask an adult to help you prepare this recipe. Wash your hands with soap and water before you begin.

You will need:

- $1^1/_2$ cups all-purpose flour
- $2/_3$ cup sugar
- $1/_2$ cup yellow cornmeal
- 1 tablespoon baking powder
- $1/_2$ teaspoon salt
- $1^1/_4$ cups milk
- 2 eggs, lightly beaten
- $1/_3$ cup vegetable oil
- 3 tablespoons butter or margarine, melted

Preheat the oven to 350 degrees. Grease an 8-inch-square baking pan. Combine flour, sugar, cornmeal, baking powder, and salt in a medium bowl. Combine milk, eggs, vegetable oil, and butter in a small bowl; mix well. Add to the flour mixture; stir just until blended. Pour into the prepared baking pan. Bake for 35 minutes or until a wooden toothpick inserted in the center comes out clean.

The Choctaw sweetened their food with honey. Drizzle honey over this warm bread for a delicious snack!

were skilled at arts and crafts. They made baskets, pottery, and decorative beadwork. From berries and wild roots they made colorful dyes to decorate crafts and clothing.

Children learned the Choctaw way of life by watching and helping adults. Children had chores to do, such as collecting water and firewood or gathering nuts and berries. Girls helped their mothers and older sisters. Boys hunted and fished with their fathers and the other men of the tribe. The boys also learned how to become good warriors. Adults often warned children that if they did not behave, tiny spirits would come and steal the children away.

During summer the Choctaw wore little clothing. Women wore skirts made from plant fibers, deerskin, or, later, cloth. Men dressed in **breechcloths**, usually made from deerskin. During winter men wore deerskin leggings and shirts. Women wore long dresses and deerskin shawls. Children wore smaller versions of the adults' clothing. In warm weather the Choctaw went barefoot. In cold weather or while hunting they wore deerskin moccasins.

Choctaw Moccasins

Choctaw men sewed deerskin moccasins for themselves and their families, which they wore in cold weather. Men also wore them while hunting. You can make your own moccasins out of felt. Ask an adult for help.

You will need:

- Brown paper bag
- 1 yard (0.9 meters) of felt, in any color
- Ruler
- Pencil
- Scissors
- Straight pins
- Needle
- Thread
- Beads in different colors (You can buy beads at craft or hobby stores.)

1· Cut the brown paper bag along one side. Cut off the bottom. Spread out the bag flat on the floor.

2· Step on the bag. Measure 4 inches (10 centimeters) out from your foot in every direction and draw an outline of this big foot. Repeat with your other foot. Cut out the paper-bag patterns.

3. Pin the patterns to the felt and cut the felt in the shape of the big feet.

4. For the first moccasin, fold the felt foot shape in half lengthwise. Sew the heel from the fold up to the opening. Repeat with the other felt foot shape.

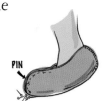

5. Place your foot inside one of the felt "feet." Pull the sides up over the top of your foot. Pin the felt along the top, leaving enough room to get your foot in and out of the moccasin. Repeat with the other felt "foot."

6. Remove your foot (be careful of the pins!) and sew along the seam. Trim off the extra felt close to the stitches.

7. For each moccasin, turn the felt inside out and turn down the flaps.

8. Glue or sew on the beads to decorate your moccasins.

Wear your moccasins and share what you have learned about the Choctaw with others.

Most Choctaw men had flattened foreheads. As infants, they were strapped to **cradleboards**. The straps pressed against their foreheads as the bones grew, which caused their foreheads to flatten. Choctaw men wore their hair long. Women also had long hair, and wore combs made from shell, bone, antler, or, later, copper. They also sometimes wore beads or flowers in their hair.

Choctaw women made strings of beads like these.

Choctaw men and boys tattooed themselves. Young men received special tattoos when they reached adulthood or became warriors. Some Choctaw men pierced their noses and wore jewelry made of bear claws. When preparing for battle some men painted their faces with red, white, or black markings.

Men wore eagle or other birds' feathers on their heads. Men who were leaders of the tribe wore feathered headdresses. Sometimes they also wore collars made of dyed horsehair. Shells, bones, and beads were made into necklaces, bracelets, and earrings for both men and women.

This museum display shows a Choctaw man in typical clothing and decoration.

3 · CHOCTAW BELIEFS

The Choctaw worshipped many different spirits. The sun was the major spirit. The Choctaw also believed that spirits lived in people, animals, and nature. They believed each person had both an inner spirit and an outer spirit. The inner spirit was called *shilup*. The outer spirit was called *shilombish*. The Choctaw thought dreams were the outer spirit's nighttime activities. Shamans and medicine men (there were also a few medicine women) were highly respected members of the tribe. Choctaw asked for their help to figure out what the dreams meant.

Medicine men and medicine women also performed chants and ceremonies to heal the sick or injured. They kept pouches with herbs and other plants that aided healing. The

The Choctaw believed that many spirits lived in nature.

pouches also contained sacred, or holy, objects, such as pipes and rattles.

The Choctaw performed **rituals** to please the spirits. Rituals to give thanks to the spirits followed births, marriages, and deaths. Choctaw hunters and warriors prayed to the spirits for success in the hunt and in battle.

Dancing was a large part of Choctaw life. Dances were performed to celebrate harvests, festivals, religious ceremonies, and weddings. The Green Corn Festival was held to give thanks for the most important crop. The festival lasted a week to two weeks. The Eagle Dance was performed before going to war. Twelve to sixteen warriors painted their bodies with white clay. Each dancer wore an eagle feather in his hair and held the tail feathers of an eagle. They danced around spears stuck in the ground.

The Choctaw usually chose their own spouses, but sometimes parents arranged marriages. Men had only one wife at a time, and most couples stayed together for life. Some couples lived in their own homes, though other couples lived with either the bride's or the groom's parents.

Although the Choctaw were often busy around the camp, they still had time to play many games. A favorite game was *toli*, an early form of lacrosse. Two teams of as many as one hundred men each moved a ball across a long field with wooden sticks that had a net on one end. Players caught the ball in the nets of their sticks and threw it between goalposts to

The Choctaw game of *toli* was an early form of lacrosse.

score. Men, women, and children played dice games using dried corn kernels or fruit seeds.

A popular Choctaw game was *chunkey*. It was played outdoors. A smooth, round disc made of stone was rolled along the ground. Two players threw long, pointed poles at the stone. The winner was the player whose pole landed closest to the stone when it finally stopped.

When a Choctaw died, the tribe believed that the shilup (inner spirit) traveled to the afterworld. The shilombish (outer

Choctaw perform the ritual of preparing a dead person's bones for burial.

spirit) stayed at home until the funeral. After the funeral, the shilombish faded away. The shilombish would not fade away for a long time if the person had been troubled in life, or had been murdered. (Today, the Choctaw word *shilup* means "ghost." The word *shilombish* means "soul.")

Ceremonies to honor the dead were held in the village. When a well-respected tribal member died, speeches were given to remember the person and to honor his or her life.

Before burial the body was placed on a scaffold, or platform. After a while a man or woman called a bone picker removed the skin from the bones. The bones were placed in burial baskets, which were placed inside bone houses. After the arrival of European **missionaries**, the Choctaw dug graves for the dead. Poles were set up around the graves. On the poles, people hung wreaths and other objects that were believed to help the spirit on its journey to the afterworld.

Each year, family members set aside a day to mourn those who had died. They marked the day by **fasting** and covering their heads.

How the Choctaw Came to Be

The Choctaw have many different creation stories. One creation story says that two brothers named Chata and Chicksah led the first people away from a land far in the West where they could no longer live. The people traveled for a long time, guided by a magical pole. Each night when the people stopped to rest, the pole was placed in the ground. The next morning, the people would travel in the direction in which the pole was leaning.

The people traveled this way for a long time. One morning, after the people had rested overnight, they saw that the pole remained upright. So the people stayed where they were. They buried the bones of their ancestors, which they had been carrying in sacks made from buffalo skins. A mound called Nanih Waiya—the Mother Mound—grew out of that burial. Located near what is now Noxapater, Mississippi, Nanih Waiya is a sacred site to the Choctaw.

Soon after settling there, however, Chata and Chicksah decided that there were too many people to live on the land. Chicksah took half the people and went to the North. They became the Chickasaw people. Chata and the others remained near the mound and became known as the Choctaw.

This Native American burial mound, located in Mississippi, is similar to Nanih Waiya, the sacred mound of the Choctaw.

4 · A CHANGING WORLD

Congress passed the Indian Reorganization Act in 1934. This law was a plan to improve the economy and lives of Native Americans throughout the country. The law called for some land to be returned to Native American tribes and it encouraged them to preserve their tribal customs and native languages by passing them on to their children.

In 1975 Congress passed the Indian Self-Determination and Education Assistance Act. It enabled tribes to rule themselves with help provided by the U.S. government. The help provided was mostly financial. The tribes used the money to build schools and tribal headquarters, and to set up community businesses.

Today about 80,000 Choctaw live in the United States, mostly in Oklahoma, Mississippi, Alabama, and Louisiana.

The Great Seal of the Choctaw Nation is an important tribal symbol.

They live as most other Americans do: they work, shop, travel, and have hobbies. They live in the modern world. But they still practice many of their traditional ways. They maintain their language, beliefs, and unique identity as Choctaw.

Education is important to the Choctaw. Since the early 1800s they have organized their own system of schools, colleges, and universities to teach their young people and prepare them to be successful.

This Choctaw child is learning the Choctaw language from her uncle. Education like this helps to keep the Choctaw culture alive.

The Indian Reorganization Act granted Native Americans the right to govern themselves. The Choctaw Nation of Oklahoma and the Choctaw Nation of Mississippi have their own constitutions. They elect leaders to represent them at tribal councils. Tribal councils consist of members who serve four-year terms. The Choctaw Nation of Oklahoma's tribal council consists of twelve members. The tribal council of the Choctaw Nation of Mississippi has sixteen members. Along with a chief, an assistant chief, and other officers, the councils make important decisions about education, employment, health care, and the economy.

Most Choctaw are members of the Choctaw Nation of Oklahoma. They live in the southeastern part of the state. They do not have a reservation. Their tribal headquarters is located in Durant, Oklahoma. A chief, an assistant chief, and the tribal council run their government. The Oklahoma Choctaw provide their members with a variety of services, including health care, education, housing, and employment. They operate many businesses, including a resort hotel and

The Choctaw Nation Casino is located in Calera, Oklahoma.

several casinos, a coliseum where major entertainers perform, and an arena where rodeos and horse shows are held. The Oklahoma Choctaw keep up with tribal news through the tribal newspaper, *Bishinik*. Each year in May, tribal members gather to participate in the Trail of Tears Walk. They re-create a portion of the journey of their ancestors to Indian Territory. The Choctaw Nation of Oklahoma also hosts yearly reunions and **powwows**.

The 8,300 tribal members of the Mississippi Band of Choctaw Indians live on 30,000 acres (12,140 hectares) in central Mississippi. Their land makes up the Pearl River Indian Reservation. The tribe owns and operates manufacturing

Members of the Mississippi Band of Choctaw Indians celebrate the opening of a new restaurant in Philadelphia, Mississippi.

and service businesses, as well as a large shopping center and a tourist resort, casino, and golf course.

The Jena Band of Choctaw Indians lives in Jena, Louisiana. There are fewer than three hundred members of this band. They do not have a reservation. Their community is well organized, however. It includes departments of housing, transportation, environment, education, and health that ensure the well-being of the members of the band. Annual tribal activities include a Choctaw Princess Pageant, Christmas parties, Thanksgiving and Valentine's Day banquets, and tribal meetings.

The MOWA Band of Choctaw Indians lives on the 300-acre (121-hectare) MOWA Choctaw Reservation in southwestern Alabama. ("MOWA" stands for the counties of Mobile and Washington, where the band lives.) There are about six thousand Choctaw living on ten small settlements.

Today's Choctaw live in the modern world while preserving their Native American heritage.

They are descendants of the Choctaw who refused to move after the 1830 Treaty of Dancing Rabbit Creek. There are five officers and fourteen members of the tribal council who make important decisions for the tribe.

Each year, during the third weekend of June, they hold a cultural festival on the reservation. The celebration includes dancing, stickball games, and a powwow that is attended by members of other Choctaw tribes. The gatherings of these and other Choctaw offer the people a chance to touch the past as they embrace the future.

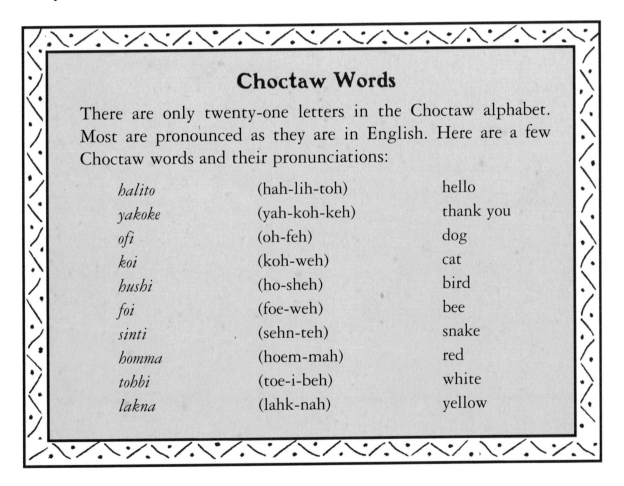

Choctaw Words

There are only twenty-one letters in the Choctaw alphabet. Most are pronounced as they are in English. Here are a few Choctaw words and their pronunciations:

halito	(hah-lih-toh)	hello
yakoke	(yah-koh-keh)	thank you
ofi	(oh-feh)	dog
koi	(koh-weh)	cat
hushi	(ho-sheh)	bird
foi	(foe-weh)	bee
sinti	(sehn-teh)	snake
homma	(hoem-mah)	red
tohbi	(toe-i-beh)	white
lakna	(lahk-nah)	yellow

· TIME LINE

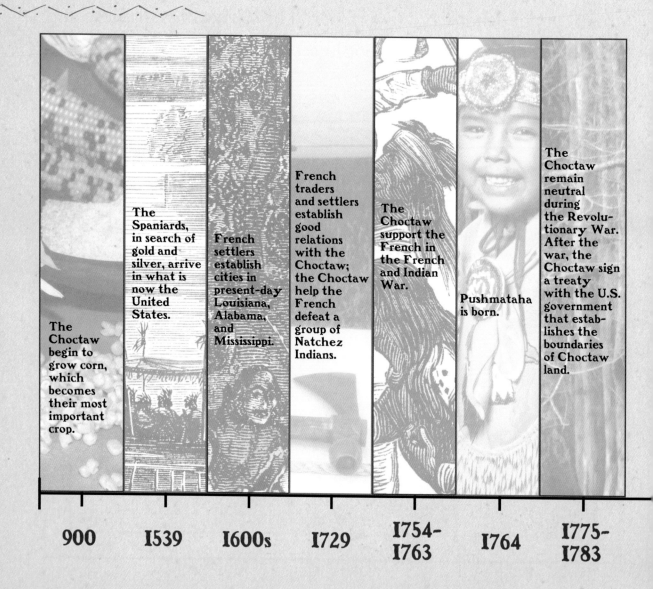

The Choctaw begin to grow corn, which becomes their most important crop.

The Spaniards, in search of gold and silver, arrive in what is now the United States.

French settlers establish cities in present-day Louisiana, Alabama, and Mississippi.

French traders and settlers establish good relations with the Choctaw; the Choctaw help the French defeat a group of Natchez Indians.

The Choctaw support the French in the French and Indian War.

Pushmataha is born.

The Choctaw remain neutral during the Revolutionary War. After the war, the Choctaw sign a treaty with the U.S. government that establishes the boundaries of Choctaw land.

900   1539   1600s   1729   1754–1763   1764   1775–1783

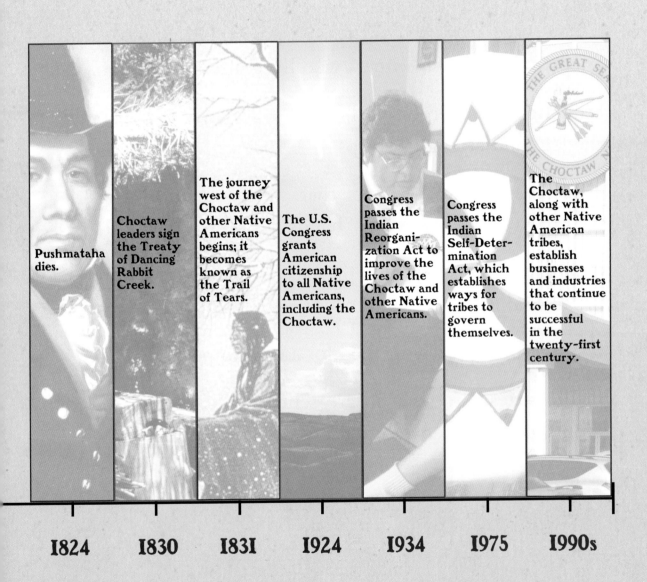

Pushmataha dies.

Choctaw leaders sign the Treaty of Dancing Rabbit Creek.

The journey west of the Choctaw and other Native Americans begins; it becomes known as the Trail of Tears.

The U.S. Congress grants American citizenship to all Native Americans, including the Choctaw.

Congress passes the Indian Reorganization Act to improve the lives of the Choctaw and other Native Americans.

Congress passes the Indian Self-Determination Act, which establishes ways for tribes to govern themselves.

The Choctaw, along with other Native American tribes, establish businesses and industries that continue to be successful in the twenty-first century.

1824   1830   1831   1924   1934   1975   1990s

· GLOSSARY

ancestors: Family members who lived a long time ago.

breechcloths: Skin or cloth garments worn by men between the legs and around the hips.

cradleboards: Baby carriers that were strapped on mothers' backs, leaving the mothers' hands free to work.

diplomat: A person who represents his or her country or people in dealings with other countries or peoples.

fasting: Going without food for a certain period of time.

missionaries: People who are sent by a church or religious group to teach their religion to others.

moats: Deep, wide ditches dug all around a village and filled with water as protection against attacks.

pelts: Skins of animals with the hair or fur still on them.

powwows: Native American social gatherings that include traditional dances.

rituals: Actions that are always performed in the same way as part of a religious ceremony or social custom.

shamans: Holy people who used spiritual powers to see the unknown, to control events, or to heal the sick.

· FIND OUT MORE

Books

Ditchfield, Christin. *The Choctaw*. Danbury, CT: Children's Press, 2005.

Gray-Kanatiiosh, Barbara A. *Choctaw*. Edina, MN: ABDO Publishing, 2007.

McKee, Jesse O. *The Choctaw*. New York: Chelsea House Publishers, 2004.

Sonneborn, Liz. *The Choctaws*. Minneapolis: Lerner Publications, 2006.

Web Sites

http://www.choctawnation.com
This is the official Web site of the Choctaw Nation of Oklahoma. It includes information about their history, culture, festivals, and a link to the *Bishinik* newspaper.

http://www.choctaw.org

Here you will find more about the Mississippi Band of Choctaw Indians, including a time line of Choctaw history and information about Choctaw treaties with the U.S. government.

http://www.jenachoctaw.org

This is the official Web site of the Jena Band of Choctaw Indians. Here you will find more about the history of the band, as well as its tribal support programs.

About the Author

Sarah De Capua is the author of many books, including biographical, geography, and historical titles. She has always been fascinated by the earliest inhabitants of North America. In this series, she has also written *The Cherokee*, *The Cheyenne*, *The Comanche*, *The Iroquois*, *The Shawnee*, and *The Shoshone*. Born and raised in Connecticut, she has also lived in Colorado and now resides in Georgia.

· INDEX

Page numbers in **boldface** are illustrations.